Dedicated to Winston,
a miniature donkey who is the best friend,
minister, and colleague and to all the miniature
donkey pet therapy teams who understand this.

Pet Partners™
Sharing the love of therapy animals

Pet Partners mission is to improve human health and well-being through the human-animal bond. As a leader in the field, Pet Partners is continuously evolving to meet the diverse needs of global communities, with innovative programming, activities, and educational opportunities that are centered around the human-animal bond. Humans and animals share a deep, innate connection, and we believe that through the human-animal bond we can improve the physical, social, and emotional lives of more people and communities.

Paperback ISBN: 979-8-9899154-2-2

Hardcover ISBN: 979-8-9899154-1-5

eBook ISBN: 979-8-9899154-0-8

Also available on Kindle.

Stay, Winston!

Words by
Ashley Cooper

Illustrations by
Zoe Saunders

Winston was a miniature donkey who loved to visit people.

He enjoyed making them smile and laugh
with his cute face and funny antics.

Winston and his mom planned to be a Pet Partners animal therapy team with the Pet Partners program so that he could visit hospitals, schools, and nursing homes.

Winston had a lot of friends in
the program, like Willow, the dog.

They all had one thing in common: they knew how to "stay" at the
end of the lead when their handler asked them to.

Winston, however, had a problem.

He did not like to stay still. He was always curious and eager to explore new places and meet new people.

He would want to follow his mom and not stay in place and wait for her to return to his side.

This made his mom, Ashley, very frustrated. She tried to teach him how to stay, but Winston did not seem to care.

One day, Ashley told Winston that he had to pass a test in order to visit people.

He had to demonstrate that he could stay at the end of his lead for at least one minute without moving or making noises.

If he failed, he would not be allowed to go on any visits.

Winston was shocked and scared. He did not want to lose his friends or his favorite activity. He loved visiting people and making them happy.

He decided that he would try his best to learn how to stay.

Ashley took him to a park where they practiced every day. She would put him on a lead and tell him to stay. Then she would walk to the end of his lead and watch him from a distance.

Winston tried hard to stay still, but it was not easy.

There were so many distractions:
squirrels, birds, children, bikes,
cars, and dogs.

Winston wanted to visit them all.

He also wanted to follow Ashley wherever she went.

He did not like being alone,
even at the end of his lead.

Ashley was patient and gentle with him. She praised him when he stayed for a few seconds and gave him treats and hugs.

She also corrected him when he moved or made noise and told him to try again.

She explained to him why staying was important: it was for his safety and for the comfort of the people he visited.

Some people might be afraid of him or allergic to him if he got too close or touched them without permission.

Some people might also be in pain or need rest and not want to be disturbed by a donkey.

Winston slowly began to understand and improve.

He learned to ignore the distractions and focus on Ashley's voice and commands.

He learned to trust her and know that she would always come back to him. He learned to enjoy the quiet moments when he could relax and watch the world go by.

After two weeks of practice, Winston was ready for his test.

Ashley took him to a special place where they met with an evaluator who would judge his performance.

The evaluator asked Ashley to put Winston in a "stay."

Ashley asked Winston to "stay" and walked to the end of his lead.
Then, the evaluator timed him with a stopwatch.

Winston felt nervous but determined. He remembered everything that Ashley had taught him and did his best to stay still and quiet. He ignored the other animals and people and focused on the evaluator's face.

He counted the seconds in his head:

one, two, three...

He made it!

He stayed without
moving or making a noise!

The evaluator smiled
and gave him a thumbs up.

She said that Winston had passed
the test and congratulated him.

Winston was overjoyed!

He ran over to Ashley and she gave him a big hug.
Winston leaned into Ashley, hugging her back.

Ashley told him how proud she was of him.
She said that he had worked hard and learned well.

Winston was happy and proud too. He had learned how to stay at the end of his lead and passed the test. Now, he could visit different kinds of people and make them happy.

He thanked Ashley for teaching him and helping him.
He also thanked the evaluator for giving him a chance.

Then he asked Ashley if they could go visit some people right away. Ashley laughed and said yes.

They left together, with Winston trotting happily on his lead.

The End

About the Author

Ashley Cooper lives with her spouse Jenny in Lewisburg, Tennessee, where they are surrounded by animals on a small farm.

Ashley received her doctorate from Lipscomb University in 2023, with her thesis' focus on the God-human-animal bond. She is an ordained minister commissioned as a community chaplain by the Federation of Christian Ministries.

Ashley loves living a simple and contemplative life, which includes taking her dogs and donkeys for walks, journaling, volunteering, reading, and camping.

www.ingramcontent.com/pod-product-compliance
Lightning Source LLC
Chambersburg PA
CBHW041428090426
42741CB00002B/82